Medicare Untangled

By Karen Emma

Introduction

Choosing the best Medicare plan is one of the most important financial decisions that you will make for your retirement years.

It isn't easy to do. Financing your retirement is at stake.

As healthcare costs continue to increase, and as we live increasingly longer, the total price you pay for Medicare will likely become more than you anticipated.

Understanding Medicare's tangle of moving parts, numerous complex rules, and continuous changes is a major challenge for anyone. That challenge is further complicated by the chronic government gobbledygook that has been befuddling people since the federal government started Medicare more than 50 years ago.

Universal Wealth Management is dedicated to providing a transparency window that enables you to see through Medicare's tangled web. This transparency is a key part of our development of the Financial Longevity Bundle© for successful retirement.

Medicare Untangled will assist you in understanding this complex program.

We will walk you through the moving parts of Medicare. This includes a simplified understanding of Medicare Parts A, B, C and D and all areas combined to formulate Medicare plans and their costs. We explain to you which healthcare costs are covered and which are not. We strive to simplify the total cost, the obvious costs, and the costs that are not so apparent.

We are here to assist you to decide which Medicare plans you really need, and help you determine which you can truly afford.

Social Security, Medicare, Centers for Medicare and Medicaid Services (CMS), and your insurance company have many rules and regulations. These details, along with continuously changing rules and regulations, are overwhelming and confusing. Ensuring that your Medicare choices fit with your retirement budget is crucial so that you do not outlive your money. Understanding the entire Medicare tangle is a must to ensuring your financial longevity.

Our goal is that *Medicare Untangled* will simplify the Medicare process for you. Should you have any questions or would like additional information visit **www.Universalwm.com** or contact us at **UWM: 401-331-7600.**

Karen Emma
President / Founder
Universal Wealth Management

Understanding the Medicare Tangle

Table of Contents

Part I

Healthcare Unscrambled:

Social Security and Medicare Simplified

Daily news reports, government announcements, and many advisory memos are often filled with head spinning gobbledygook.

Here, we simplify a number of healthcare terms into clear language.

Social Security
Programs first created by Congress in 1935 and now composed of Old-Age, Survivors and Insurance (OASDI), Medicare, Medicaid, and various grants-in-aid, which provide economic security to nearly all those employed.

Medicare
A national healthcare insurance program which originated in 1965, primarily for Americans age 65 and older who worked and paid a

payroll tax matched by their employer. Some people under age 65 can qualify because of disabilities or health conditions including End-Stage Renal Disease (also known as ESRD), permanent kidney failure requiring dialysis or transplant.

Medicare Has Four (4) Parts:

Medicare Part A (Hospital Insurance)
Hospital, skilled nursing facility care, nursing home care (as long as custodial care is not the only care you need), home healthcare and hospice services. Managed by the federal government. Most people do not pay a premium for Part A.

Medicare Part B (Medical Insurance)
Outpatient services such as doctor's visits, preventative care, surgeries, lab work, X-rays, durable medical equipment (DME) such as wheelchairs, walkers, oxygen equipment or blood testing strips for diabetics; *limited* prescription drugs and many other services considered medically necessary. You pay a premium for Part B.

You are required to pay deductibles for Medicare Part A and B before Medicare will start to cover your healthcare services. You also will be responsible for paying coinsurance — usually 20% — of the charges for many services of Original Medicare.

Medicare Part C (Also known as Medicare Advantage)
Original Medicare is one option within Part C, in which you can piece together your overall coverage by coordinating your plan to cover any uncovered charges in Original Medicare (Part A & B). This is often known as Supplemental Medical Insurance (SMI) or Medigap. Medicare Part C is the part of Medicare law that allows private health insurance companies to provide Medicare benefits. These are insurance plans that you can purchase to help cover coinsurance, deductibles and copays.

You can purchase Part C in two ways:

**Option 1: Original Medicare (Part A & B)
(Medicare Supplement / Medigap)**

This includes Medicare Part A & B. You can add and/or piece this together to coordinate uncovered charges in Medicare Part A and B (Original Medicare) by purchasing an individual insurance Medigap or Medicare Supplemental insurance plan for Part C as well as an individual insurance plan to cover Part D for Medicare prescription drug coverage.

Option 2: Medicare Advantage Plan (Part C)

You can also purchase a Medicare Advantage Plan which includes all Parts A, B, C and D in one packaged Medicare insurance plan.

- Medicare Advantage Plans (Part C) provide coverage within Part C of Medicare and are available through private insurance companies that have contracts with the Federal Government.

- The Part C monthly premium varies by plan along with the copays and by healthcare companies.

Medicare Part D (Prescription Drug Coverage)

Medicare Part D, Prescription Drug Coverage, is an insurance plan which helps Medicare beneficiaries pay for their prescription drugs / medications. Whether you have a stand-alone Medicare Prescription Drug Plan, or you get your Part D coverage as part of a Medicare Advantage Plan, it works the same way. Your plan has a list of covered drugs, called a formulary.

- The covered drugs are divided into Tiers. You pay the same copay or coinsurance for all the drugs in each Tier. For example, you might pay a $3 copay for a Tier 1 drug, but you might pay 25% coinsurance for a Tier 4 drug.

- Prescription Drug Plan costs can vary based on individual insurance companies. Deductibles may apply.

- Specific Drug Tiers medications can vary based on individual plans.

- The drug cost itself along with the copays and/or coinsurance percentages can also vary with each plan.

- It is imperative that you review your medication list when picking a prescription drug plan. Variations among companies and plans can be costly.

Affordable Care Act (ACA)

The Affordable Care Act was created to make affordable health insurance available to more people. The law provides consumers with subsidies ("premium tax credits") that lower costs for households with incomes between 100% and 400% of the federal poverty level.

Annual Enrollment Period (AEP)
(October 15th - December 7th)

Also known as Medicare Open Enrollment, Annual Election Period or Annual Coordinated Election Period. This is the time during which Medicare plan enrollees can reevaluate their coverage, whether it's Original Medicare with supplemental drug coverage, or Medicare Advantage, and make changes to your plans. AEP is always held October 15th - December 7th. Any changes will be effective January 1st.

Assignment

An agreement by your doctor, provider, or supplier to be paid directly by Medicare, to accept the payment amount Medicare approves for the service, and not to bill you for any more than the Medicare deductible and coinsurance.

Benefit Period

The way that Original Medicare measured your use of hospital and skilled nursing facility (SNF) services. A benefit period begins the day you're admitted as an inpatient in a hospital or SNF. The benefit period ends when you haven't received any inpatient hospital care (or skilled nursing care in a SNF) for 60 consecutive days. If you go into a hospital or a SNF after one benefit period has ended, a new benefit period begins. You must pay the inpatient hospital deductible for each benefit period. There's no limit to the number of benefit periods.

Catastrophic Health Insurance - High Deductible Health Plans (HDHPs)

An insurance policy with a lower premium based on a high deductible and possibly narrower coverage if available.

Centers for Medicare & Medicaid Services (CMS)

Medicare is managed by the Centers for Medicare & Medicaid Services (CMS). Social Security works with CMS by enrolling people in Medicare. CMS is part of the U.S. Department of Health and Human Services (HHS). CMS oversees many federal healthcare programs, including those that involve health information technology such as the meaningful use incentive program for electronic health records (EHR).

Children's Health Insurance Program (CHIP)

Insurance program jointly funded by state and federal government that provides health insurance to children in families that do not qualify for Medicaid but earn enough to purchase private insurance.

Co-Payment

An amount you may be required to pay as your share of the cost for a medical service or supply such as a doctor's visit, hospital outpatient visit, or a prescription drug. A copayment is usually a set amount, rather than a percentage.
Example: you might pay $10 or $20 for a doctor's visit.

Coinsurance (Percentage Participation)

An amount you may be required to pay as your share of the cost for services after you pay any deductibles. Coinsurance is usually a percentage.
Example: The insurance company may agree to pay 80% of the insured expenses with the insured paying the other 20%.

Conditional Payment

A payment Medicare makes for services another payer may be responsible for. Medicare makes this conditional payment so you won't have to use your own money to pay the bill. The payment is "conditional" because it must be repaid to Medicare if you get a settlement, judgement, award or other payment later. You are responsible for making sure Medicare gets repaid from the settlement, judgement, award or other payment.

Consolidated Omnibus Budget Reconciliation Act (COBRA)

Consolidated Omnibus Budget Reconciliation Act of 1985, extending group health coverage to terminated employees and their families for up to 18 or 36 months.

Continuing Care

Type of health or medical care designed to provide a benefit for elderly individuals who live in a retirement community. It addresses full-time needs, both social and medical. Also known as residential care.

Coordinated Care Plans (CCP)

Coordinated Care Plans are Medicare Advantage plans or Medicare Health plans that offer healthcare through an established provider network and are approved by the Centers for Medicare and Medicaid Services (CMS). Medicare Advantage plans that are classified as Coordinated Care Plans include: HMOs (Health Maintenance Organizations); HMO-POS (HMOs with a Point of Service option); PPOs (Preferred Provider Organization which include local and regional PPOs) and SNPs (Medicare Advantage Special Needs Plans).

Coordination of Benefits (COB)

Provision designed to prevent duplication of group insurance benefits. It limits benefits from multiple group health insurance policies in a particular case to 100% of the expenses covered. The COB provision also designates the order in which the multiple carriers are to pay the benefits.

Cost of Living Adjustment (COLA)

A cost-of-living adjustment is made to Social Security and Supplemental Security Income (SSI) offsetting the effects of inflation. Cost-of-living adjustments (COLAs) are typically equal to the percentage increase in the Consumer Price Index for a specific period. Social Security and Supplemental Security Income (SSI) benefits for more than 69 million Americans will increase 2.6 percent in 2020.

Creditable Coverage

Creditable coverage is a health insurance, prescription drug, or other health benefit plan that meets a minimum set of qualifications. Types of creditable coverage plans include: group health plan; individual health insurance; student health insurance; Medicare; Medicaid; CHAMPUS and TRICARE; the Federal Employees Health Benefits Program (FEHBP); Indian Health Service; the Peace Corps; Public Health Plan (any plan established or maintained by a State, the U.S. government or a foreign country); Children's Health Insurance Program (CHIP); or a state health insurance high risk pool. If you have prior creditable coverage, it will reduce the length of a pre-existing condition exclusion period under new job-based coverage. Creditable coverage is used to determine coverage and costs associated with pre-existing conditions, and whether policyholders have to pay late enrollment penalties.

Custodial Care

Non-skilled personal care, such as an aid to help with activities of daily living. It may also include the kind of health-related care that

most people do themselves such as using eye drops or taking pills. In most cases, Medicare does not pay for custodial care.
Examples: bathing, dressing, eating, getting in or out of bed or chair, moving around and using the bathroom.

Deductibles
An amount that must be paid before a Medicare insurance payment is initiated.

Dual Eligible
Individuals who are eligible for both Medicare & Medicaid.

Full Dual Eligible
Individuals who are entitled to Medicare Part A and Part B and receive full Medicaid benefits.

Partial Dual Eligible
Other dual eligible beneficiaries, referred to as "partial dual eligible beneficiaries," do not receive Medicaid benefits directly. Instead, Medicaid provides "Medicare Savings Programs" through which beneficiaries receive assistance with some or all of their Medicare premiums, deductibles and other cost-sharing requirements.

Durable Medical Equipment (DME)
Equipment and supplies ordered by a healthcare provider for everyday or extended use. Typically, DME may be considered a separate category under a health insurance plan. Coverage for DME may include oxygen equipment, wheelchairs, walkers, crutches or blood testing strips for diabetics.

If your supplier accepts assignment, you pay 20% of the Medicare-approved amount, and the Part B deductible applies. Medicare pays for different kinds of DME in different ways.

Depending on the type of equipment:

- You may need to rent the equipment.

- You may need to buy the equipment.

- You may be able to choose whether to rent or buy the equipment.

Medicare will only cover your DME if your doctors and DME suppliers are enrolled in Medicare. Doctors and suppliers have to meet strict standards to enroll and stay enrolled in Medicare. It's also important to ask your suppliers if they participate in Medicare before you get DME. If suppliers are participating suppliers, they must accept assignment. If suppliers are enrolled in Medicare but aren't "participating," they may choose not to accept assignment. If suppliers don't accept assignment, there's no limit on the amount they can charge you.

Exclusive Provider Organization (EPO)
A type of plan in which a member of an EPO can use the doctors and hospitals within the EPO network but cannot go outside the network for care. There are no out-of-network benefits.

Explanation of Benefits (EOB)
The statement arrives via mail by an insurance company and closely resembles a medical bill. The EOB provides details about a medical insurance claim that has been in process and explains what portion was paid to the healthcare provider and what portion of the payment, if any, is the responsibility of the patient. **The EOB is not a bill.** Any portion of the medial expense not covered by the insurance company such as a deductible or copay will be billed by the provider and should be paid directly to the provider.

Extra Help
A Medicare program to help people with limited income and resources to pay Medicare prescription drug program costs, such as premiums, deductibles and coinsurance. **Also known as Low Income Subsidy (LIS).**

Federal Poverty Level (FPL)

A measure of income issued every year by the Department of Health and Human Services. They are used to determine your eligibility for certain programs and benefits including health insurance, Medicaid and Children's Health Insurance Program (CHIP).

Flexible Spending Account (FSA)

Accounts offered and administered by employers that allow employees to put money into the account on a pre-tax basis to cover certain out of pocket medical expenses. FSA withdrawals are tax free when used for medical expenses, prescriptions, dental, deductibles and copays but not for insurance premiums. The employer may also contribute to this account. Typically, benefits must be used in a given benefit year or the employee loses the money.

Formulary

Medicare-approved lists of prescription drugs by a prescription drug plan or another insurance plan offering prescription drug benefits.

General Enrollment Period
(January 1st – March 31st)

The General Enrollment Period is the time period between January 1st and March 31st of every year when you can enroll in Medicare Part B for the first time. If you enroll during this period (and it is after your Initial Enrollment Period), your coverage will begin on July 1st.

Guaranteed Issue Rights

Rights you have in certain situations when insurance companies are required by law to sell or offer you a Medigap policy. In these situations, an insurance company can't deny you a Medigap policy, or place conditions on a Medigap policy, such as exclusions for pre-existing conditions. They also cannot charge you more for a Medigap policy because of a past or present health problem.

Health Care Reform (HCR)

Also known as the Patient Protection and Affordable Care Act (PPACA), the Affordable Care Act (ACA) and Obamacare. It is the comprehensive healthcare reform law enacted in March 2010. The law was enacted in two parts: PPACA was signed into law on March 23, 2010. It was amended by the Health Care and Education Reconciliation Act on March 30, 2010. Health Care Reform refers to the final, amended version of the law.

Health Insurance Portability and Accountability Act (HIPAA)

A US law designed to provide privacy standards to protect patients' medical records and other health information provided to health plans, doctors, hospitals and other health care providers. Developed by the Department of Health and Human Services (HHS), these new standards provide patients with access to their medical records and more control over how their personal health information is used and disclosed. They represent a uniform, federal floor of privacy protections for consumers across the country. State laws providing additional protections to consumers are not affected by this new rule. HIPAA took effect on April 14, 2003.

Health Maintenance Organizations (HMO)

HMO plans offer a wide range of healthcare services through a designated network of providers who agree to supply services to members. With an HMO you will likely have coverage for a broader range of preventive healthcare services than you would through another type of plan. An HMO plan may require referrals from a primary care physician in order to see a specialist. It is important to know that you may not have coverage for services rendered by out-of-network providers or for services rendered without a proper referral from your PCP (Primary Care Physician).

Health Savings Account (HSA)

A Health Savings Account (HSA) allows you to set aside money on a pre-tax basis to pay for qualified medical expenses. It is available to taxpayers in the United States who are enrolled in a high-deductible health plan (HDHP). The funds contributed to an account are not subject to federal income tax at the time of deposit. By using untaxed dollars in a Health Savings Account (HSA) to pay for deductibles, copayments, coinsurance, and some other expenses, you can lower your overall healthcare costs.

High-Deductible Health Plan (HDHP)
A plan with a higher deductible than a traditional insurance plan. The monthly premium is usually lower, but you pay more health care costs before the insurance company starts to pay its share (your deductible). A high deductible plan (HDHP) can be combined with a health savings account (HSA), allowing you to pay for certain medical expenses with money free from federal taxes.

In-Network
In-network refers to providers or healthcare facilities contracted to be covered by an insurance policy. They are part of a health plan's network for which these providers or healthcare facilities have negotiated a discount. Insured individuals usually pay less when using an in-network providers. Healthcare providers are contractually required to care for patients who possess specific insurance policies. It is important to understand that in-network providers have agreed to accept the insurance company's payment (plus the patient's pre-determined cost-sharing amount) as payment in full. However, out-of-network providers do not have a contractual agreement with the insurer. Out-of-network providers can and do charge patients the remainder of the fee after the insurance company has paid its share. (Some policies are not restricted).

Inpatient Hospitalization
Necessary admission status of a patient to qualify for Medicare Part A insurance coverage. Copays are based on the Medicare Plan you've selected.

Initial Coverage Election Period (ICEP)

ICEP is the period during which those who are newly eligible for Medicare Part A & B can enroll in a Medicare Advantage plan. During the ICEP, you can enroll in a Medicare Advantage health plan with or without prescription drug coverage.

- The applicant is new to Medicare and is in their 7 month initial election period and electing to enroll into a plan with NO RX coverage (MA only),

   OR

- The applicant delayed their Part B when first eligible. They are enrolling into Part B after the expiration of the Initial Enrollment Period (IEP) and are requesting to enroll in a MA / MAPD plan in the 3 months prior to their Part B effective date.

Initial Enrollment Period (IEP)

When you're first eligible for Medicare, you have a 7-month Initial Enrollment Period to sign up for Part A and/or Part B.

Example: If you are eligible for Medicare when you turn 65, you can sign up during the 7 month period that:

- Begins 3 months before the month you turn 65

- Includes the month you turn 65

- Ends 3 months after the month you turn 65

Long-Term Care (LTC)

Services that include medical and non-medical care provided to people who are unable to perform basic activities of daily living such as dressing or bathing. Long-term support and services can be provided at home, in the community, in assisted living, or in nursing homes. Individuals may need long-term care support and services at any age. Medicare and most health insurance plans don't pay for long-term care.

Long-Term Disability (LTD)

Long-term disability refers to an injury, illness, or accident that keeps a person from working for a long period of time. The definition of long-term disability (and the time period over which coverage extends) differs among insurance companies and employers. Long-term disability insurance is usually purchased in conjunction with short-term disability insurance and typically kicks in after the benefits of the short-term policy expire. Long-term disability insurance coverage does not provide insurance for work-related accidents or injuries that are covered by workers compensation insurance. It does cover an employee in the event of a personal accident such as a car accident or a fall. Long-term disability insurance policies ensure that an employee will still receive a percentage of their income if they cannot work due to sickness or a disabling injury. Long-term disability policies typically pay at a reduced rate, usually 50 to 70 percent of the insured's regular pay rate for an extended period of time that may last from several years to the life of the insured.

Low Income Subsidy (LIS)

Eligible beneficiaries who have limited income may qualify for a government program that helps pay for Medicare Part D prescriptions drug costs. Medicare beneficiaries receiving the low-income subsidy (LIS) get assistance in paying for their Part D monthly premium, annual deductible, coinsurance, and copayments. Also, individuals enrolled in the Extra Help program do not have a gap in prescription drug coverage (Medigap). The amount of subsidy depends on the individual's income compared to the Federal Poverty Level (FPL) and resource limitations set by the Social Security Act. Also known as Extra Help.

Medicaid

A joint federal and state program originated in 1965, Medicaid helps with medical costs for some people with limited income and resources. Medicaid can provide free or lower-cost health insurance plans for low income and disabled US citizens and legal permanent residents. Medicaid programs can vary from state to state, but most healthcare costs are covered if you qualify for both Medicare and Medicaid. The Affordable Care Act (ACA), also known as Obamacare, expanded Medicaid to include applicants with incomes 133% over the poverty line.

Medical Savings Account (MSA)

Medical Savings Account plans deposit tax deferred deposits into a "healthcare checking account" that individuals use to pay healthcare costs before the deductible is met. Withdrawals from the MSA are tax-free if used to pay for qualified medical expenses. The MSA must be coupled with a high-deductible health plan (HDHP). Withdrawals from MSA go toward paying the deductible expenses in a given year. MSA account funds can cover expenses related to most forms of healthcare, disability, dental care, vision care, and long-term care, whether the expenses were billed through the qualifying insurance or otherwise.

Medical Underwriting

The process that an insurance company uses to decide, based on your medical history, whether to accept your application for insurance; whether to add a waiting period for pre-existing conditions (if your state law allows it); and how much to charge you for that insurance.

Medicare Advantage (MA)

Medicare Plans sometimes called "Part C" are an "all in one" alternative to Original Medicare. They are offered by private companies approved by Medicare instead of the federal government. These plans typically include the same Part A hospital, Part B medical coverage and Part D drug coverage that Medicare covers, with the exception of hospice care. Some Medicare Advantage Plans also offer coverage of vision, dental and hearing. Enrollment in Medicare Advantage Plans has nearly doubled over the past decade. As of 2019, about 64 million people are enrolled in Medicare. One third (⅓) of all Medicare beneficiaries (approximately 22 million) are enrolled in Medicare Advantage Plans.

Medicare-Approved Amount
In Original Medicare, this is the amount a doctor or supplier who accepts the assignment can be paid. It may be less than the actual amount a doctor or supplier charges. Medicare pays part of this amount and you're responsible for the difference.

Medicare Payroll Tax
A 2.9% tax on employees' salaries throughout their working lifetime. The tax expense is split between the employee and employer. The self-employed pay the entire 2.9%. Earned income exceeding $200,000 is taxed at 3.8%. The Medicare Payroll Tax is a premium used to finance Medicare.

Modified Adjusted Gross Income (MAGI)
Modified Adjusted Gross Income (MAGI) represents your adjusted gross income (AGI) plus certain deductions. Your AGI is your gross income less any allowable deductions such as for retirement plan contributions, student loan interest and health insurance premiums paid by self-employed individuals. MAGI is the figure used to determine eligibility for lower costs in the Health Insurance Marketplace / Health Insurance Exchange (HIM/HIX) and for Medicaid and CHIP. This number is used also to determine your Medicare Part B premium. Generally, MAGI is your AGI plus any tax-exempt Social Security, interest, foreign income, foreign housing deductions, student-loan deductions, IRA contribution deductions and deductions for higher-education costs you may have.

National Drug Code (NDC)
The National Drug Code (NDC) is a system used to identify unique drug products in the United States intended for human use. An NDC number for a specific product is created by the FDA and the manufacturer to ensure that products can be differentiated; no currently marketed products may have the same NDC number.

Open Enrollment Period (OEP) – Medicare Advantage (January 1st – March 31st)

The Open Enrollment Period returned as of January 2019. It has replaced the election period known as Medicare Advantage Disenrollment Period (MADP). In the Open Enrollment Period beneficiaries currently enrolled in Medicare Advantage can switch to another Medicare Advantage plan with or without drug coverage and disenroll from a Medicare Advantage plan with or without drug coverage and return to Original Medicare. If you do so you will be able to join a Medicare prescription drug plan. You can also enroll or cancel a stand-alone Part D prescription drug plan. Medicare Advantage Open Enrollment Period is held annually January 1st – March 31st. Any changes made during the Medicare Advantage Open Enrollment Period become effective as of the 1st of the following month.

Open Enrollment Period for Institutionalized Individuals (OEPI)

The OEPI is continuous for eligible individuals who meet the definition of "institutionalized" to enroll or disenroll from a Medicare Advantage Special Needs Plan for institutionalized individuals.

Out-of-Pocket (OOP)

This can include deductibles, copayments and/or coinsurance, along with payments for Medicare Part D prescriptions.

Over the Counter (OTC)

Referring to a medical drug or device that can be purchased by a consumer without a doctor's prescription.

Out-of-Network (OON)

Out-of-Network refers to physicians, hospitals or other healthcare providers who do not participate in an insurer's provider network. This means that the provider has not signed a contract agreeing to accept the insurer's negotiated prices. Depending on an individual's health insurance plan, expenses incurred for services provided by out-of-plan health professionals may not be covered, or they may only be partially covered by an individual's insurance company. Plans that cover out-of-network care are less common than in the past, but they are still available in many areas. They generally impose a higher deductible and out-of-pocket limit (or even no upper limit) when patients obtain care from an out-of-network provider. It is important to understand that out-of-network providers can and do bill patients for the remainder of the charges after the insurance company has paid its share. In-network providers have agreed to accept the insurance company's payment (plus the patient's pre-determined cost-sharing amount) as payment in full, but out-of-network providers have not signed any sort of agreement with the insurer.

Outpatient Services

Medical services outside hospital admission that qualify for Medicare Part B insurance coverage. These services are procedures or tests that can be done in a medical center without an overnight stay. Many can be done in a few hours. Outpatient services include: Wellness and prevention, such as counseling and weight-loss programs; Diagnosis, such as lab tests and MRI scans; Treatment, such as some surgeries and chemotherapy; Rehabilitation, such as drug or alcohol rehab and physical therapy.

Patient-Centered Medical Home (PCMH)

The patient-centered medical home is a model of care that puts patients at the forefront of care. PCMHs are designed to build better relationships between patients and their clinical care teams. Research shows that PCMHs improve quality, the patient experience and increase staff satisfaction — while reducing health care costs. Practices that earn recognition have made a commitment to continuous quality improvement and a patient-centered approach to care. PCMHs are held accountable for meeting the large majority of each patient's physical and mental health care needs, including prevention and wellness, acute care, and chronic care while providing comprehensive care required with a team of care providers. These teams might include physicians, advanced practice nurses, physician assistants, nurses,

20

pharmacists, nutritionists, social workers, educators, and care coordinators. Although some medical home practices may bring together large and diverse teams of care providers to meet the needs of their patients, many others, including smaller practices, will build virtual teams linking themselves and their patients to providers and services in their communities.

Pharmacy Benefit Management (PBM)

Health plans and sponsors contract with Pharmacy Benefit Managers to handle the claims processing and administrative functions involved with prescription drug programs. In addition to processing and paying claims, PBMs develop and maintain a program drug formulary, contract with participating pharmacies and negotiate discounts and rebates with drug manufacturers.

Point of Service (POS)

POS plans have some of the qualities of HMO and PPO plans with benefit levels varying depending on whether you receive your care in or out of the health insurance company's network of providers. Like an HMO plan, you may be required to designate a Primary Care Physician (PCP). Referrals are required from your PCP for specialist visits. Services rendered by your PCP are typically not subject to a deductible depending upon the plan. Preventive care benefits are usually included. Like a PPO plan, you may receive care from non-network providers but with that comes greater out-of-pocket costs. You may also be responsible for copayments, coinsurance and an annual deductible.

Pre-Existing Condition (PEC)

A health problem such as asthma, diabetes, or cancer that you had before the date that new health coverage starts. Under current law, health insurance companies can't refuse to cover treatment for your pre-existing condition or charge you more. These rules went into effect for plan years beginning on or after January 1, 2014. There is one exception to the pre-existing coverage rule, which is that it does not apply to "grandfathered" individual health insurance policies. A grandfathered individual health insurance policy is a policy that you bought for yourself or your family on or before March 23, 2010 that has not been changed in certain specific ways that reduce benefits or increase costs to consumers.

Pre-Existing Condition Insurance Plan (PCIP)

The Pre-existing Condition Insurance Plan (PCIP) ended on April 30, 2014. The PCIP program provided health coverage options to individuals who were uninsured for at least six months, had a pre-existing condition, and had been denied coverage (or offered insurance without coverage of the pre- existing condition) by a private insurance company. Currently due to the Affordable Care Act, health insurance plans can no longer deny anyone coverage for their pre-existing condition, and so PCIP enrollees can transition to a new plan outside of the PCIP program.

Preferred Provider Organization (PPO)

Preferred Provider Organization plans are one of the popular types of Medicare Advantage plans. PPO plans allow you to visit whatever in-network physicians or healthcare providers are in an established network. These plans are likely to cover more of your medical costs if you stay inside that network. You do not need a referral from your primary care physician to see a specialist. No matter which healthcare provider you choose, in-network healthcare services will be covered at a higher benefit level than out-of-network services.

Premiums

An annual amount charged for Medicare Parts B and D; also, C if utilized, and healthcare insurance for people under the age of 65.

Primary Care Physician (PCP)

The primary physician who coordinates your care. Your Primary Care Physician makes sure you get the care you need to keep you healthy. Your PCP also may talk with other doctors and healthcare providers about your care and refer you to them. In many Medicare Advantage Plans, you must see your primary care physician before you see any other healthcare provider.

Private Fee-for-Service (PFFS)

Private Fee-for-Service plans are Medicare Advantage plans that allow you to receive care from any hospital or doctor that accepts the plan's coverage. The plan does not have to follow Medicare guidelines when it comes to paying for the services you receive. It can cost more or less than Medicare. However, these plans often offer more coverage than Original Medicare. Private fee-for-service plans sometimes include prescription drug coverage, but, if they don't, you're allowed to purchase a stand-alone prescription drug plan - that's not the case with other Medicare Advantage plans. You do not need to choose a Primary Care Physician (PCP) under PFFS plans, and you do not need a referral to get specialist care. It is important to ask in advance if your provider accepts the payment terms under a PFFS plan to avoid any unexpected expenses.

Qualified Health Plan (QHP)

An insurance plan that is certified by the Health Insurance Marketplace and meets ACA requirements. A QHP provides essential health benefits and follows established limits on cost-sharing (such as deductibles, copayments, and out-of-pocket maximum amounts), and meets other requirements under the Affordable Care Act. All qualified health plans meet the Affordable Care Act requirement for having health coverage, known as Minimum Essential Coverage.

Short-Term Disability (STD)

Short-term disability refers to an injury or illness that keeps a person from working for a short time. The definition of short-term disability (and the time period over which coverage extends) differs among insurance companies and employers. Short-term disability insurance coverage is designed to protect an individual's full or partial wages during a time of injury or illness (that is not work-related) that would prohibit the individual from working. Short-term disability typically becomes effective within 14 days of the insured becoming disabled, according to the Insurance Information Institute. The policy may pay a significant percentage of the insured's regular pay rate, up to 90 percent, for a period of up to two years.

Skilled Nursing Facility Care (SNF)

Skilled nursing care and rehabilitation services provided on a continuous, daily basis in a skilled nursing facility. Examples include physical therapy or intravenous injections that can only be given by a registered nurse or doctor.

Social Security Disability Income (SSDI)

Social Security Disability Insurance is funded through payroll taxes. SSDI recipients are considered "insured" because they have worked for a certain number of years and have made contributions to the Social Security trust fund in the form of FICA Social Security taxes. SSDI candidates must be younger than 65 and have earned a certain number of "work credits." There is a five-month waiting period for benefits, meaning that the Social Security Administration (SSA) won't pay you benefits for the first five months after you become disabled. The amount of the monthly benefit after the waiting period is over depends on your earnings record. After receiving SSDI for two years, a disabled person will become eligible for Medicare.

Special Election Period (SEP)

Also known as Special Enrollment Period. A SEP is a time period during which Medicare beneficiaries can change their Medicare Advantage or Part D coverage outside of the normal annual open enrollment period and after their initial enrollment period has ended. A special election period will be triggered by a qualifying event, which can include a move from the area covered by a recipient's existing Medicare plan, loss of other coverage, a violation of policy terms by a plan provider or other reasons approved by the Centers for Medicare and Medicaid Services. There are special election periods for Medigap as well (known as "guaranteed issue rights"), but they are re more limited, and Medigap does not have an annual open enrollment period.

Special Needs Plans (SNP)

Medicare Special Needs plans are a type of Medicare Advantage plan that provides all of the health care and services of Medicare Parts A and B to people who require special care for chronic illnesses, care management of multiple diseases, and focused care management. These plans may be limited to individuals in specific types of institutions - such as nursing homes - or beneficiaries who are dual eligible (both Medicare / Medicaid eligible), or who have specific chronic or disabling conditions.

Specialty Pharmacy Provider (SPP)

A national specialty pharmacy provider offering comprehensive specialty drug management services focused on improving care and outcomes for patients living with complex conditions. Specialty pharmacy providers may provide home health or nursing services.

State Health Insurance Assistance Program (SHIP)

A state program that receives money from the Federal Government to provide free local health insurance counseling to people with Medicare.

State Supplementary Payment (SSP)

State supplementary payments are any payments made by a State or one of its political subdivision (including any such payments for which reimbursement is available from the Social Security Administration (SSA) to a recipient of supplemental security income benefits (SSI). There are two types of State Supplementary Payments: mandatory and optional. A SSP is mandatory if you were converted to SSI from a State assistance program, your State must supplement the SSI amount. The amount of the supplement is what is necessary to provide you the same level of payment you had before you were converted to SSI. Payments may be issued directly by the State or the State may elect Federal administration where the mandatory payment and the SSI payment are combined in one payment by the Federal Government. Optional SSP are provided by most States to SSI recipients. These payments vary from State to State and reflect differences in regional living costs. SSP may be made directly by the State or combined with the SSI payment (by mutual agreement of SSA and State agencies).

Summary of Benefits and Coverage (SBC)
Summary of Benefits and Coverage (SBC) provides individuals with standard information so they can compare medical plans as they make decisions about which plan to choose.

Supplemental Security Income (SSI)
A federal governmental program that provides monthly benefits to people who are age 65 or older, blind, or disabled and who have low income and limited resources. SSI is strictly need-based, according to income and assets, and is funded by general fund taxes. This is not from the Social Security trust fund. SSI is called a "means-tested program," meaning it has nothing to do with work history, but strictly with financial need. To meet the SSI income requirements, you must have less than $2,000 in assets (or $3,000 for a couple), limited face value of life insurance and a very limited income. Disabled people who are eligible under the income requirements for SSI are also able to receive Medicaid in the state they reside in. Most people who qualify for SSI are eligible for medical assistance, homemaker, and other services, such as food stamps (SNAP benefits), hearing aids, discounts on telephone and electric bills, and the assistance of a social worker. The amount an eligible person will receive is dependent on where they live and the amount of regular, monthly income. SSI benefits will begin on the first of the month when you first submit your application.

Tiers
Insurance co-pay coverage payment levels within a formulary. The amount you pay depends on what tier your medication is grouped. This varies based on individual insurance companies and the specific drug/medication. It is imperative to check your medication list against your plan's formulary and review how they are tiered. Variations among companies can be costly. Copayment / Coinsurance costs can change at any time.

Part II

Medicare Overview Made Simple

H ealthcare today is one of the largest expenditures in most retirement budgets. Costs continue to rise. For your retirement plan, it is more important than ever that you have a clear understanding of Medicare's current complexities, not just now but when the **Annual Medicare Open Enrollment Period (October 15th - December 7th)** approaches.

With this knowledge, you are better able to evaluate Medicare plans and make smart adjustments to meet your healthcare needs at the lowest possible cost.

Medicare is a federal government health insurance program for most people age 65 or older; also, for some people under age 65 who qualify because of disabilities or health conditions such as End-Stage Renal Disease (ESRD). Medicare is managed overall by the Centers for Medicare & Medicaid Services (CMS). Social Security works with CMS by enrolling people in Medicare and collecting Medicare premiums.

Medicare, itself, is divided into four parts:

- Medicare Part A (Hospital Insurance)
- Medicare Part B (Medical Insurance)
- Medicare Part C (Medicare Advantage)
- Medicare Part D (Prescription Drug Coverage)

Medicare Part A (Hospital Insurance)

- Medicare Part A covers inpatient hospital stays, care in a skilled nursing facility (as long as custodial care is not the only care you need), hospice care and home healthcare.

- Medicare Part A has its own set of coverage costs: copays, coinsurance, deductibles and possibly late enrollment penalties.

- Most people usually do not pay a monthly premium for Medicare Part A coverage (sometimes called "premium-free Part A") if you or your spouse paid Medicare taxes while working.

- You also can receive premium-free Medicare Part A at 65 if:

  ➤ You already get retirement benefits from Social Security or the Railroad Retirement Board.

  ➤ You're eligible for Social Security or Railroad benefits but haven't filed for them yet.

  ➤ You or your spouse had Medicare-covered government employment.

  ➤ If you're under 65, you can get premium-free Medicare Part A if:

    o You received Social Security or Railroad Retirement Board disability benefits for 24 months.

o You have End-Stage Renal Disease (ESRD) and meet certain requirements.

Medicare Part B (Medical Insurance)

- Medicare Part B covers outpatient care such as doctor's visits, surgeries, durable medical supplies (DME) (such as wheelchairs, walkers, oxygen equipment or blood testing strips for diabetics), preventive care, X-rays, lab work, **limited** prescription drugs and many other services considered medically necessary to treat a disease or condition.

- Some people automatically get Medicare Part B (Medical Insurance). Others need to sign up for Part B. If you don't sign up for Part B when you're first eligible, you may have to pay a late enrollment penalty.

- You pay a premium for Medicare Part B. If you receive Social Security, Railroad Retirement Board, or Office of Personnel Management benefits, your Part B premium may be automatically deducted from your benefit payment. If you don't receive these benefit payments, you'll get a bill directly from Centers for Medicare & Medicaid Services (CMS).

Reminder: Medicare is managed by the Centers for Medicare & Medicaid Services (CMS). Social Security works with CMS by enrolling people in Medicare. The Centers for Medicare and Medicaid Services (CMS) is part of the U.S. Department of Health and Human Services. CMS oversees many federal healthcare programs, including those that involve health information technology such as the meaningful use incentive program for electronic health records (EHR).

- Most people will pay the standard monthly premium in 2020 of $144.60 (or higher depending on your income). This is an increase of $9.10 from 2019. Medicare uses the Modified Adjusted Gross Income (MAGI) reported on your IRS (Internal Revenue Service) tax return from two (2) years ago (the most recent tax return information provided to Social Security by the IRS).

- If your modified adjusted gross income is above a certain amount, you may pay an increased amount in your Medicare Part B premium costs, also known as Income Related Monthly Adjustment Amount (IRMAA).

- Medicare Part B has its own set of coverage costs: copays, coinsurance, deductibles and late enrollment penalties.

Medicare Part C (Medicare Advantage)

- Medicare Part C covers uncovered Medicare A & B costs for such services as primary care office visits, specialist office visits, inpatient medical hospitalization, skilled nursing facilities, outpatient surgery, diagnostic tests (X-Rays, MRIs, PET Scans, and various lab services), home healthcare, emergency room visits and ambulance services.

Medicare Advantage Plans (Part C)

A Medicare Advantage Plan is a type of health plan offered by a private insurance company that contracts with Medicare to provide you with Parts A, B, C and D, all in one plan. Medicare Advantage plans pay for managed healthcare based on a monthly fee per enrollee, rather than on the basis of billing for each medical service provided for unmanaged healthcare services. Medicare Advantage plans finance at a minimum the same medical services as Original Medicare - Parts A and B. This is financed via a fee-for-service. Part C plans, including Medicare

Advantage plans, also typically finance additional services, such as health services in addition to those covered under Part A & B, and most importantly include an annual out of pocket spending limit not included in Parts A and B. A Medicare Advantage beneficiary must first sign up for both Part A and Part B of Medicare. These plans are designed to reduce co-pays, coinsurance, and deductibles associated with Original Medicare benefits.

- Medicare Advantage Plans include Health Maintenance Organizations (HMO), Preferred Provider Organizations (PPO), Private Fee-for-Service Plans (PFFS), Special Needs Plans (SNP) and Medicare Medical Savings Account (MSA) Plans.

- If you're enrolled in a Medicare Advantage Plan, most Medicare services are covered through the plan as your primary insurance, with Original Medicare acting as a secondary plan.

- Medicare Advantage Plans have a monthly premium which varies by plan and insurance companies.

Medicare Supplemental Plans

Medicare Supplemental Plans are types of health plans offered by a private insurance company that contracts with Medicare to provide you with supplemental coverage to Part A and Part B. These plans are designed to reduce or eliminate co-pays, coinsurance and deductibles associated with Original Medical benefits.

- If you're enrolled in a Medicare Supplemental Plan, most Medicare services are covered by Original Medicare as your primary insurance, with the Supplemental Plan acting as a secondary plan.

- Medicare Supplemental Plans do not offer prescription drug coverage (see Medicare Part D). You would have to purchase Part D separately.

- Medicare Supplemental Plans have a monthly premium which varies by plan and insurance companies. Some plans are based on your age when you are first issued coverage.

Medicare Part D (Prescription Drug Coverage)

- Medicare Part D adds prescription drug coverage to Original Medicare Parts A and B for drugs which are not included under Part B.

- Medicare Part D coverage is offered by insurance companies and other private companies approved by Medicare, either as a stand-alone plan or as part of a Medicare Advantage Plan.

- Medicare Advantage Plans may also offer prescription drug coverage that follows the same rules as Medicare Prescription Drug Plans.

- The Medicare Part D monthly premium varies by plan (higher- income consumers may pay more). Medicare uses the Modified Adjusted Gross Income (MAGI) reported on your IRS tax return from two (2) years ago (the most recent tax return information that the IRS provides to Social Security).

- If your modified adjusted gross income is above a certain amount, you may pay an increased amount in your Part D premium costs, also known as Income Related Monthly Adjustment Amount (IRMAA).

- Having Medicare Part D coverage is optional, but it is important to understand that you may have to pay the federal government a penalty for enrolling late.

- You can avoid the penalty if you already have prescription drug coverage that is at least as good as Medicare Part D through another health plan, such as an employer or union retiree plan, the Veterans Administration, or TRICARE (the civilian care component of the Military Health System).

- Medicare Part D has its own set of coverage costs based in each individual plan. Copays, coinsurance, deductibles and late enrollment penalties vary.

Part III

Medicare Enrollment Periods Made Simple

edicare Part A & Part B Sign Up Periods

1. **Initial Enrollment Period (when you are first eligible for Medicare)**

   - You have a seven (7) month Initial Enrollment Period to sign up for Medicare Part A and/or Part B.

   - If you're eligible for Medicare when you turn 65, you can sign up during the seven (7) month period that:

      ➢ Begins three (3) months before the month you turn 65

      ➢ Includes the month you turn 65

      ➢ Ends three (3) months after the month you turn 65

   - Coverage start date depends on your birthday.

      ➢ Your coverage starts the first day of the month that

you turn 65, unless your birthday is on the first day of the month. (***Example:*** Mr. Brown's 65th birthday is August 8. He can begin to sign up for Medicare in May. His effective coverage will begin on August 1).

➤ If your birthday is on the first day of the month, your coverage starts the first day of the prior month. (***Example:*** Mr. Green's 65th birthday is July 1. He can begin to sign up for Medicare in March. His effective coverage begins on June 1).

- If you are eligible for Medicare, you can sign up for premium-free Medicare Part A any time during or after your Initial Enrollment Period starts. Your coverage start date will depend on when you sign up.

- If you have to buy Part A and/or Part B, you can only sign up during a valid enrollment period.

- If you wait to enroll until the month you turn 65 (or the three (3) months after you turn 65), your Part B coverage will be delayed. This could cause a gap in your coverage.

- In most cases, if you don't sign up for Medicare Part B when you are first eligible, you'll have to pay a late enrollment penalty, an increase in your premium that you will have to pay as long as you have Part B.

2. General Enrollment Period (January 1 – March 31)

- The General Enrollment Period is the time period between January 1st and March 31st of every year when you can enroll in Medicare Part B for the first time.

- If you enroll during this period (and it is after your Initial Enrollment Period), your coverage will begin on July 1.

- If you weren't automatically enrolled in Medicare, and you missed your IEP, you can still apply for Medicare Part A and/or Part B during the General Enrollment Period.

- In most cases, if you don't sign up for Medicare Part B when you are first eligible, you'll have to pay a late enrollment penalty, an increase in your premium that you will have to pay as long as you have Part B.

3. **Annual Open Enrollment Period (October 15 - December 7)**

Here is what you can do:

- Change from Original Medicare to a Medicare Advantage Plan.

- Change from a Medicare Advantage Plan back to Original Medicare.

- Switch from one Medicare Advantage Plan to another Medicare Advantage Plan.

- Switch from a Medicare Advantage Plan that doesn't offer drug coverage to a Medicare Advantage Plan that offers drug coverage.

- Switch from a Medicare Advantage Plan that offers drug coverage to a Medicare Advantage Plan that doesn't offer drug coverage.

- Join a Medicare Prescription Drug Plan.

- Switch from one Medicare drug plan to another Medicare drug plan.

- Drop your Medicare prescription drug coverage completely.

4. **Medicare Advantage Open Enrollment Period (New in 2019) (January 1 - March 31 annually)**

- The original Medicare Advantage Disenrollment Period (January 1st – February 14th every year) has been replaced with a different arrangement, now called Medicare Advantage Open Enrollment Period.

- If you're enrolled in a Medicare Advantage plan, you'll have a one-time opportunity to:

  - ➤ Switch to a different Medicare Advantage plan.

  - ➤ Drop your Medicare Advantage plan and return to Original Medicare, Part A and Part B.

  - ➤ Sign up for a stand-alone Medicare Part D Prescription Drug Plan (if you return to Original Medicare). Most Medicare Advantage plans include prescription drug coverage already. Usually you can't enroll in a stand-alone Medicare Prescription Drug plan if you already have a Medicare Advantage plan, but in some situations you can.

- You can sign up for Medicare Part A and/or Part B during the Medicare Advantage Open Enrollment Period if:

  - ➤ You didn't sign up when you were first eligible.

  - ➤ You aren't eligible for a Special Enrollment Period (SEP). *(See below for SEP details)*

- You must pay premiums for Medicare Part A and/or Part B. **Your coverage will begin July 1** – not immediately as many people believe.

- You may have to pay a higher premium for late enrollment in Medicare Part A and/or Part B.

- If you don't have Medicare or you want to sign up for Medicare Part A, we invite you to **contact us now** at **UWM: 401-331-7600 or www.Universalwm.com** so that our experts may help you navigate through the Social Security system process.

- If you also want to sign up for Medicare Part B, we can simplify the process. **Contact us immediately** at **UWM: 401-331-7600 or www.Universalwm.com** to learn more.

- UWM can provide application forms and instructions in English, Spanish and many other languages upon request.

5. **Special Enrollment Periods (SEP) - Special Circumstances**

- Once your Initial Enrollment Period ends, you may have the chance to sign up for Medicare during a Special Enrollment Period (SEP). If you're covered under a Group Health Plan based on current employment, you have a SEP to sign up for Medicare Part A and/or Part B anytime as long as:

  ➢ You or your spouse (or family member if you're disabled) is working.

  ➢ You're covered by a Group Health Plan through your employer or union based on that employment.

    o A Group Health Plan is generally a health plan offered by an employer or employee organization that provides health coverage to employees and their families.

- You also have an eight (8) month SEP to sign up for Medicare Part A and/or Part B that begins if either of the following happens first:

  ➢ The month after employment ends.

  ➢ The month after your group health plan insurance based on current employment ends.

- If you sign up during a SEP, you usually don't pay a late enrollment penalty.

  ❖ **BEWARE:**

    ➢ **COBRA and Retiree Health Plans aren't considered coverage based on current employment.** You're not eligible for a Special Enrollment Period (SEP) when employment coverage ends. This SEP also doesn't apply to people with End-Stage Renal Disease (ESRD).

➢ If you have a **Health Savings Account (HSA) with a High Deductible Health Plan (HDHP)** based on you or your spouse's current employment, you may be eligible for a SEP. To avoid a tax penalty, you should stop contributing to your HSA at least six (6) months before you apply for Medicare.

➢ You can still withdraw money from your HSA after you enroll in Medicare to help pay for medical expenses (like deductibles, premiums, coinsurance or copayments).

➢ You may also qualify for a SEP for Medicare Part A and Part B if you're a volunteer serving in a foreign country.

➢ Medicare coverage start dates can vary for each individual and are dependent on various factors such as your birth month, special circumstances, employment and enrollment periods.

➢ Failure to enroll in Medicare during appropriate enrollment periods can cost you long-lasting, varying penalties.

Part IV

Medicare Part A & Part B Costs and Penalties

Medicare Part A (Hospital Insurance) – Covers inpatient hospital stays, care in a skilled nursing facility (as long as custodial care is not the only care you need), hospice care and home healthcare.

Medicare Part A coverage includes semi-private rooms, meals, general nursing, drugs as part of your inpatient treatment, and other hospital services and supplies received in these facilities: acute care hospitals, critical access hospitals, inpatient rehabilitation facilities and long-term care hospitals.

Medicare Part A coverage also includes inpatient care as part of a qualifying clinical research study; also inpatient mental healthcare given in a psychiatric hospital or other hospital.

❖ **BEWARE:**

Here are some examples of services that are **not covered** by Medicare Part A:

➢ Private-duty nursing.

➢ Private room (unless medically necessary).

➢ Television and phone in your room (if a separate charge applies for these items).

➢ Personal care items such as razors or slipper socks.

Medicare Part A: Premium Cost

You **usually do not pay a monthly premium** for Medicare Part A if you or your spouse paid Medicare payroll taxes throughout either of your working life.

❖ **BEWARE:**

➢ If you paid Medicare taxes for less than 30 quarters, you pay a standard monthly premium of $458 in 2020 compared to $437 in 2019.

➢ If you worked more than 30 to 39 quarters, the standard monthly premium would be reduced to $252 in 2020 compared to $240 in 2019.

Medicare Part A: Hospital Deductibles and Coinsurance

1. You pay a **deductible** for each benefit period when admitted to a hospital. Many Medicare patients are not aware of this deductible. In 2020, the deductible was set at $1,408 compared to $1,364 in 2019.

2. You begin to pay **coinsurance** for each benefit period after your first 60 days in a hospital or skilled nursing facility.

3. Benefit periods are broken down by days in the hospital or skilled nursing facility:

- Days 1-60: $0 coinsurance for each benefit period. (Same as 2019)

- Days 61-90: $352 coinsurance per day for each benefit period compared to $341 in 2019.

- Days 91 and beyond: $704 coinsurance per each "lifetime reserve day" after day 90 for each benefit period (up to 60 days over your lifetime). It was $682 in 2019.

- Beyond lifetime reserve days: You pay all the costs directly.

  ❖ **BEWARE:**

  ➤ All people with Medicare Part A are covered for inpatient hospital care when all of these conditions are met:

    o You must be admitted by the hospital. It requires a doctor to make an official order that says you need two or more 24-hour periods of medically necessary treatment for your illness or injury.

    o You need the kind of care that can be given only in the hospital.

    o The hospital must accept Medicare.

    o The hospital Utilization Review Committee approves your stay in the hospital. **You are not eligible just by being in an Emergency Room or under observation.** That would then be covered by Medicare Part B, and includes varying deductibles, copays and coinsurance.

Medicare Part A: Late Enrollment Penalty (LEP)

❖ **BEWARE:**

➢ Your monthly premium can go up 10% if you do not enroll in Medicare when first eligible at age 65 due to the Part A Late Enrollment Penalty.

➢ Be sure to review the correct process in our *Financial Longevity Bundle* © *eBook - Untangling Medicare - Part III: Medicare Enrollment Periods Made Simple.* Also contact us at **UWM: 401-331-7600 or www.Universalwm.com** for more in-depth information.

Medicare Part B (Medical Insurance) - Covers outpatient care such as doctor's visits, surgeries, durable medical equipment (DME) (*Examples:* wheelchairs, walkers, oxygen equipment or blood testing strips for diabetics), preventive and screening care, X-rays, lab work, **limited** prescription drugs and many other services considered medically necessary to treat a disease or condition.

Medicare Part B: Premium Costs

- You pay a standard monthly premium of $144.60 in 2020 compared to $135.50 in 2019 (or higher depending on your income as reported on your IRS tax return from two years prior). Medicare uses the modified adjusted gross income reported on your IRS tax return from two (2) years ago (the most recent tax return information provided to Social Security by the IRS).

- If your modified adjusted gross income is above a certain amount, you may pay an increased amount in your Medicare Part B premium costs, also known as Income Related Monthly Adjustment Amount (IRMAA).

Important Note:

➤ Medicare retirees are continuing to pay more -- in many cases a lot more. In five years, individuals have experienced an increase of approximately 40% in their Medicare Part B premiums. In 2019, the standard monthly premium was $135.50. In 2020, the standard monthly premium amount increased 7% to $144.60 for single tax filers with incomes of less than $87,000, and married couples filing jointly with income of less than $174,000.

➤ For beneficiaries above these income levels, the Medicare Part B premium can climb steadily to a maximum of $491.60 for individuals earning more than $500,000 or married couples earning more than $750,000. These individuals and married couples will now be paying up to 240% more of Part B costs.

➤ Based on the new price levels, an individual with just over $85,000 in income will now be paying up to 40% of Medicare Part B costs. As income rises, so too, will your percentage of Part B costs for which you are responsible. Individuals with just over $163,000 of income will now be paying up to 220% more of Part B costs.

❖ **BEWARE:**

➤ Your standard monthly premium may vary year to year and is based on a number of factors and changes that continue surrounding Social Security, cost of living adjustments (COLA), Medicare healthcare costs, and constantly evolving standards within the Affordable Care Act (ACA) and other healthcare providers.

Medicare Part B: Deductible and Coinsurance

1. **Your annual deductible for Medicare Part B is $198 in 2020 compared to $185 in 2019.**

2. After your deductible is met, you pay coinsurance, typically 20% of Medicare approved charges.

   ❖ **BEWARE:**

   ➢ Medicare-approved amount in Original Medicare is the amount a doctor or supplier that accepts assignment can be paid. It may be less than the actual amount a doctor or supplier charges. Medicare pays part of this amount and you are responsible for the difference.

   ➢ Actual doctors, supplier and negotiated contract charges can vary. This makes it almost impossible for Medicare subscribers to know exactly how much they are paying in actual dollar budget numbers when trying to calculate the rate of 20% coinsurance of the Medicare approved charges and lists which are constantly changing.

Medicare Part B: Late Enrollment Penalty (LEP)

   ❖ **BEWARE:**

   ➢ If you do not enroll in Medicare Part B coverage when you are first eligible, your monthly premium can go up an additional 10% for each full 12-month period that you could have had Medicare Part B coverage.

➤ You may also have to wait until the Medicare Advantage Open Enrollment Period (January 1 - March 31) to enroll in Medicare Part B, which would cause your coverage to begin July 1 of that year, not immediately.

Part V

Medicare Part C – Costs, Medicare Advantage Plans vs. Supplemental Plans

Do you want additional insurance to cover some of the medical healthcare costs for Medicare? You can buy it from private insurance companies that are under contract with Medicare.

This is Medicare Part C which offers you a choice of **Two Options:**

You may choose only one of these two options:

- **Option One: Medicare Advantage Plans**

    A type of Medicare health plan offered by a private insurance company to provide you with Medicare Parts A, B, and D packaged together in one Medicare healthcare plan designed to reduce copays, deductibles and coinsurance. There are many different types of Medicare Advantage plans, described below:

➤ Health Maintenance Organizations (HMOs) require you to use healthcare providers in a designated plan network and may require referrals from a primary care physician in order to see a specialist.

➤ Point of Service (POS) plans have some of the qualities of HMO and PPO plans with benefit levels varying depending on whether you receive your care in or out of the health insurance company's network of providers. Like an HMO plan, you may be required to designate a Primary Care Physician (PCP). Referrals are required from your PCP for specialist visits. Services rendered by your PCP are typically not subject to a deductible depending upon the plan. Preventive care benefits are usually included. Like a PPO plan, you may receive care from non-network providers but with that comes greater out-of- pocket costs. You may also be responsible for copayments, coinsurance and an annual deductible.

➤ Preferred Provider Organizations (PPOs) recommend the use of "preferred" healthcare providers in an established network. These plans are likely to cover more of your medical costs if you stay inside that network. You don't need a referral to see a specialist.

➤ Private Fee-for-Service (PFFS) plans determine how much you will pay healthcare providers, and how much the beneficiary is responsible to cover out-of-pocket.

➤ Special Needs Plans (SNP) are tailored health insurance plans designed for beneficiaries with certain health conditions.

➢ Medical Savings Account (MSA) plans deposit money into a "healthcare checking account" that you use to pay for healthcare costs before the deductible is met.

- **Option Two: Medicare Supplemental Plans.**

Sometimes called Medigap or MedSup Plans, these supplemental plans cover at least the same coverage as Original Medicare copays, deductibles and coinsurance where they apply for primary care office visits, specialist office visits, inpatient medical hospitalization, skilled nursing facilities, outpatient surgery, and diagnostic tests such as x-rays, lab services, home healthcare, emergency room visits, and ambulance services. Some diagnostic tests such as MRIs and PET scans may incur additional costs.

❖ **BEWARE:**

➢ If you're enrolled in a Medicare Advantage plan or another Medicare plan, you may have different rules, but your plan must give you at least the same coverage as Original Medicare. Some services may only be covered in certain settings or for patients with certain conditions.

➢ Medicare Advantage Plans and Medicare Supplemental Plans have significant differences when it comes to costs, benefits, and how they work. It's important to understand these differences as you review your Medicare coverage options.

➢ You generally cannot enroll in both a Medicare Advantage plan and a Medigap plan at the same time.

Example 1: *Edna has a Medicare Advantage Plan (HMO). Since Edna is receiving her coverage through a Medicare Advantage plan, instead of Original Medicare, the rules for out-of-state coverage are different and will depend on the type of Medicare Advantage plan she is enrolled in. Certain types of Medicare Advantage plans, such as HMOs, have provider networks of doctors and hospitals that Edna must use to be covered for routine care. The provider network may be limited. However, Edna will still be covered if she needs emergency hospital and medical care, out-of-area urgent care, or out-of-area kidney dialysis. Edna's Medicare Advantage plan (HMO) may also require referrals from a primary care physician in order for her to see a specialist of choice.*

Example 2: *If Edna had chosen a Medicare Advantage Plan (PPO), she would have more flexibility and this may allow her to see healthcare providers outside of her plan's preferred provider network. Depending on the rules of her plan, however, she may have to pay a higher copayment or coinsurance to receive non-emergency care from an out-of-network provider.*

Example 3: *If Edna had chosen a Medicare Supplemental plan, also known as Medigap or MedSup, she would have purchased this plan through a private insurance company, but it is not comprehensive medical coverage. Instead, her Medigap functions as supplemental coverage to Original Medicare. Current Medigap plans don't include prescription drug coverage so she would have to purchase a prescription drug plan separately. Her Medigap plan may cover costs like Medicare coinsurance and copayments, deductibles, and emergency medical care while traveling outside of the United States.*

Important Note 1: *There are currently 10 standardized plan types in 47 states, each given a lettered designation (Plan C or F or G, for example). Plans of the same letter offer the same benefits regardless of where you purchase your plan. Massachusetts, Minnesota, and Wisconsin offer their own standardized Medigap plans.*

Important Note 2: *Each of the standardized Medigap plans cover certain Medicare out-of-pocket costs to at least some degree. Every Medigap plan covers up to one year of Medicare Part A coinsurance and hospital costs after Medicare benefits are used up. But, for example, Medigap Plan G plans don't cover your Medicare Part B deductible, while Medigap Plan C plans do. Compare the Medigap policies carefully.*

Important Note 3: *While benefits are standardized, the costs are not. Your costs could fluctuate depending on the insurance company offering the plan and location. That is, while Medigap Plan G includes the same coverage no matter where you buy it, the premium for this plan can vary. Also, not every standardized lettered plan is offered in every state.*

Important Note 4: *If you decided to sign up for a Medigap policy, a good time to do so is during the Medigap Open Enrollment Period, a six-month period that typically starts the month you turn 65 and have Medicare Part B. If you enroll in a Medigap plan during this period, you can't be turned down or charged more because of any health conditions.*

If you apply for a Medigap plan later on, you may be subject to <u>medical underwriting</u>; your acceptance into a plan isn't guaranteed.

If you enroll in a Medicare Advantage plan or a Medicare Supplemental plan, you must continue paying your Part B premium.

Important Note 5: (Foreign Travel) - If you are traveling outside the United States, beware that Medicare generally does not provide for care outside the U.S. There are some limited exceptions, such as care on a cruise ship while in U.S. territorial waters or emergency care that occurs while you are en route to the U.S. and the closest hospital is in another country, such as Canada. Most Medicare Advantage plans provide you with worldwide emergency coverage. If you choose one of the ten standard Medigap plans that offer Foreign Travel, most believe they can travel without worry. However, benefits may be limited and most plan are also limited to a lifetime benefit of $50,000. You must review your plan benefits if you plan to be out of the U.S. for an extended period.

Critical Details of Medicare Advantage Plans to keep in mind:

- Medicare Advantage Plans cover areas such as primary care office visits, specialist office visits, inpatient medical hospitalization, skilled nursing facilities, outpatient surgery, diagnostic such as x-rays, lab services, home healthcare, emergency room visits, and ambulance services are often provided. MRIs, PET scans, and some other diagnostic tests may incur additional costs. Most Medicare services are covered through the plan as your primary insurance with Original Medicare acting as a secondary plan.

- If you have a Medicare Advantage plan, you're still enrolled in the Medicare program; in fact, you must sign up for Medicare Part A and Part B to be eligible for a Medicare Advantage plan. The Medicare Advantage Plan administers your benefits to you. Depending on the plan,

Medicare Advantage can offer additional benefits beyond your Part A and Part B benefits above, such as routine dental, vision, and hearing services, and even prescription drug coverage. If you decide to sign up for a Medicare Advantage plan, you may want to shop around, because costs and coverage details are likely to vary. Contact us at **UWM: 401-331-7600** or visit us at **www.Universalwm.com** to help you understand all available Medicare Advantage options and coverage details.

- Medicare Advantage Plans have a monthly premium which varies by plan and insurance company. Most premium costs range up to $250. Some have no premium. Copays vary by plan.

- Most Advantage Plans include Medicare Part D (Prescription Drug Coverage) as part of the plan premium costs, but many also have deductibles.

❖ **BEWARE:**

➢ There are some Medicare Advantage Plans that do not include prescription drug coverage. This can be a costly error if you select such a plan and then do not have Part D coverage, thereby incurring late enrollment penalties and additional costs.

Example 1: *Deborah enrolled in a Medicare Supplemental Plan F. Since she was not taking medications at the time, she did not enroll in a Medicare Part D - Prescription Drug Plan (PDP). She was unaware that she was required to enroll in a PDP plan to avoid late enrollment penalties and additional costs. Two years later, Deborah was prescribed a high-end medication. When*

Deborah went to the pharmacy to pick up her prescription, she was told that since she did not have prescription plan coverage, she would have to pay full price for the medication. Deborah's only option for enrolling in a new PDP plan would have to take place during the next Medicare Open Enrollment Period. In the meantime, Deborah was forced to either pay for her prescriptions out of pocket for the remainder of the year or hold off on purchasing until her new plan was in effect.

During Medicare Open Enrollment, Deborah applied for a new prescription drug plan (PDP). She was informed that not only would she now have to pay a monthly premium for a prescription plan, she would also incur a late enrollment penalty (LEP), an additional monthly cost paid by Medicare Part D beneficiaries who did not enroll in a Medicare Part D prescription drug plan when they were first eligible - or who were without "creditable" prescription drug coverage for more than 63 days.

"Creditable drug coverage" is any prescription coverage that is at least as good as basic Medicare Part D prescription drug coverage. Some examples of creditable drug coverage include VA (Veterans Administration) drug coverage, TRICARE, or employer/union drug coverage. All of these example plans should be reviewed and checked with one's employer/union health plan administrator to verify that the drug coverage is "creditable" for purposes of Medicare Part D.

If you are subject to a late-enrollment penalty, you will pay your plan's monthly Medicare Part D premium along with an additional penalty calculated as one percent of the annual national base Medicare Part D monthly premium for each month you were without creditable prescription drug coverage. The penalty is permanent, and you will pay the penalty (adjusted each year for the annual base Medicare Part D premium) as long as you have Medicare drug coverage.

Example 2: An estimate of your 2020 Medicare Part D late-enrollment penalty

*If you were previously without creditable prescription drug coverage for five years (60 months), you would have to pay, in addition to your monthly Medicare plan premium, a monthly penalty of **$19.64** (60 months without drug coverage times 1% of $32.74 in 2020) or approximately an additional **$236** per year for your drug coverage. (Medicare calculates the penalty by multiplying 1% of the "national base beneficiary premium" ($32.74 in 2020) times the number of full, uncovered months you did not have Part D or creditable coverage. The monthly premium is rounded to the nearest $0.10 and added to your monthly Part D premium.) The national base beneficiary premium may increase each year, so your penalty amount may also increase each year. This does not include the costs for the medication itself. You may also be responsible for additional deductibles, copays and more as you will see referenced in the **Financial Longevity Bundle** © **eBook - Untangling Medicare - Part VI: Medicare Part D – Costs and Penalties of Prescription Drug Coverage.***

- **Medicare Advantage Plans have what is known as "Maximum Out-of-Pocket" - In-Network and Out-Of-Network (MOOP).**

  ❖ **BEWARE**:

  ➢ Out-of-Pocket Maximum/Limit are maximum dollar amount(s) that you could be responsible for paying. The costs can range among plans anywhere from $ 2,200 to $10,000.

  ❖ **BEWARE**:

  ➢ **In-Network and Out-Of-Network Out-Of-Pocket Maximum/Limit are two separate areas and responsibilities.**

➢ The In-Network and Out-of-Network Maximums are the maximum amount you will pay for covered medical services within a given plan year. Once you hit this threshold for deductibles, coinsurance and copayments, your health plan pays 100% for covered services from in-network providers and out-of-network providers. Premium payments are not included in your out-of-pocket maximum/limit.

➢ Plans vary on In-Network Maximum/Limit, as well as, Out-of-Network Maximum/Limit.

➢ In many plans these costs are considered separate Out-Of-Pocket expenses. They are the maximum dollar amounts you could owe separately for In or Out-Of-Network expenses.

➢ Some plans have a <u>Combined</u> In-Network and Out-of-Network Out-Of-Pocket Maximum/Limit.

Example 3: Peter is enrolled in Medicare Advantage plan (POS). POS stands for Point of Service plan and makes up only six percent of health plans. POS plans are a hybrid of PPO and HMOs. This means that Peter gets to choose whether to use HMO or POS services each time he sees a provider. Peter is usually treated in his home state of Rhode Island (RI) which allows him to have lower costs and a reasonable in-network maximum out-of-pocket expense. In Peter's case, his in-network maximum out-of-pocket is $5,000. Following multiple procedures in RI, unexpected medical issues arose for Peter. He needed a follow up surgery and it was recommended that the procedure take place in neighboring Massachusetts. Peter was subjected to additional costs since his surgery and doctors were now out-of-network. Despite the fact that Peter had already paid his $5,000 In-Network Out-Of-Pocket Maximum/Limit, he was also required to pay the Out-Of-Network Maximum/Limit of $10,000. His total costs were $15,000.

❖ **BEWARE:**

➢ Although your insurer will report all Medicare costs to you, many are unaware of these fees. If you are reasonably healthy, you do not have to pay all of the maximum costs. But, if you have an unexpected health issues, the costs may increase quickly.

❖ **BEWARE**:

➢ Many of the service categories mentioned above have significant charges by providers in addition to your out-of-pocket costs. Some costs do count against your maximums. However, this becomes meaningful to you if the maximums have not been reached, and you face major healthcare expenses. Those charges (bills) will be covered only after you pay any maximum shortfalls, and these costs can be surprisingly substantial.

➢ Many Medicare Advantage Plans have deductibles for the Part D Prescription Drug Coverage and also have varying copays and Tiers for drugs.

❖ **BEWARE**:

➢ You must review all your prescription drugs alongside the plan formularies - the official list of prescriptions drugs, both generic and brand name, used by practitioners to identify drugs that offer the greatest overall value. A committee of independent, actively practicing physicians and pharmacists maintain the formulary which can change from time to time. Checking it will ensure you know the expected costs and plan details for your prescription drug coverage.

> Medicare Advantage Plans also offers additional benefits including fitness, vision hardware and hearing aids. Sometimes these are offered free of charge or at a small monthly rate. Such benefits vary by plan and insurance company and are continuously changing and evolving.

- Medicare Advantage Plans vary by federal and state laws.

- Insurance companies make local coverage decisions in each state that processes claims for Medicare. These insurance companies decide whether something is medically necessary and/or should be covered in their area. However, Medicare makes the national coverage decisions about whether something is covered.

Critical Details of Supplemental Plans to keep in mind:

- Supplemental Plans provide you with supplemental coverage to Medicare Part A and Part B provided by Original Medicare. The supplement is designed to reduce or eliminate co-pays, coinsurance and deductibles associated with the Original Medicare benefits.

- Supplemental Plans do not offer prescription drug coverage (Medicare Part D). You must purchase Medicare Part D separately.

- Supplemental Plans have a monthly premium which varies by plan and insurance company. Some plans are based on your age when you are first issued coverage.

- You cannot have a Supplemental Plan and an Advantage Plan at the same time.

❖ **BEWARE:**

> ➤ Medicare Supplemental Plans vary by plan and by insurance company. Coverage, premiums, deductibles and rate scales are often hidden within the plans making it imperative to review your healthcare needs along with all costs.

Example 1: When Mr. & Mrs. Smith questioned a rate change at the start of the New Year on their Medicare Supplement plans. They discovered they were both paying a tobacco rate instead of a non-tobacco rate. Their previous agent had checked the wrong box. Once the correction was made, Mr. & Mrs. Smith saved $700 annually. You must pay attention to detail.

❖ **BEWARE:**

> ➤ Medicare Supplemental Plans are often more expensive and have higher monthly premiums than Medicare Advantage Plans even though they do not have copays associated with the plans. Also, medical services such as MRI, PET Scans and more could still have underlying costs. It is imperative to know your plan as well as what you can afford in your monthly budget.

❖ **BEWARE:**

> ➤ Supplemental Plans can have various names and letters differentiating the plans. These plans are offered by various insurance companies and are often called the XYZ insurance company F Plan, G Plan, H, Plan, I Plan, J Plan, K Plan, N Plan and so forth. There are many to choose from, but the names and acronyms can be confusing. Do your homework to understand the details and benefits offered within each supplemental plan.

Part VI

Medicare Part D
Costs and Penalties of
Prescription Drug Coverage

P reviously, we discussed the parts of Medicare that
provide medical benefits, but very **limited**
prescription drug coverage. However, as previously
noted, there is more expanded drug coverage in one more "part" of
Medicare that is important to your healthcare needs. This is
Medicare Part D — Prescription Drug Coverage. There are two
ways to obtain Medicare Part D coverage.

Medicare Part D (Prescription Drug Coverage) – Covers
prescription drugs not included under Part B. Coverage is available
from private insurance companies, either as a stand-alone plan or
as part of a Medicare Advantage Plan.

There are two ways to get Prescription Drug Coverage:

1. Medicare Prescription Drug Plan (Part D). These plans
   (sometimes called "PDPs") are a stand-alone plan which adds
   drug coverage to Original Medicare, some Medicare Cost

Plans, some Medicare Private Fee-for-Service (PFFS) Plans and Medicare Medical Savings Account (MSA) Plans.

2. Medicare Advantage Plan (Part C) (such as an HMO or PPO) or other Medicare health plan that offers Medicare prescription drug coverage allows you to get all of your Medicare Part A (Hospital Insurance) and Medicare Part B (Medical Insurance Coverage) and Medicare Part D (Prescriptions Drug Coverage) in one plan. Medicare Advantage Plans with prescription drug coverage are sometimes called "MA-PD" Plans. You must have Medicare Part A and B to join a Medicare Advantage Plan.

Medicare Part D: Premium Cost

- You pay a monthly premium for Medicare Part D.

- Medicare Part D monthly premiums vary by plan and drugs covered.

- Currently the average monthly premium is $34. (Could be more based on income).

- Medicare Part D prescription drug plans may have a deductible. Deductibles vary between plans. Some Medicare prescription drug plans do not have a deductible. Medicare sets a limit on the deductible for prescription drug plans each year. Plans cannot charge you more than the annual limit. In 2020, the deductible for Medicare Part D is $435, an increase from $415 in 2019.

- Medicare uses the modified adjusted gross income reported on your IRS tax return from two (2) years ago (the most recent tax return information provided to Social Security by the IRS). If your modified adjusted gross income is above a certain amount, you may pay an increased amount in your Part D premium costs, also known as Income Related Monthly Adjustment Amount (IRMAA).

- Medicare Part D coverage is optional, but you may have to pay a penalty to the federal government if you don't enroll in a Part D plan when you are eligible. This penalty can be avoided if you currently have prescription drug coverage through an employer, union retiree plan, the Veterans Administration or TRICARE. The coverage must be as good as Medicare Part D coverage.

❖ **BEWARE:**

➢ Monthly premiums vary by plan (higher-income consumers may pay more depending on your income as reported on your IRS tax return from two years prior).

➢ Most Medicare Advantage Plans include Medicare Part D (Prescription Drug Coverage) as part of the overall plan premium costs, but <u>deductibles</u> can be found in many of the plans creating additional often unexpected costs.

➢ Medicare Part D coverage, as stated, is optional if you have creditable prescription drug coverage.

Example: John is age 65. He is still working and covered under his employer healthcare plan, which includes prescription drug coverage. John may enroll in Medicare Part A, but does not need to enroll in Medicare Part B, C or D. He will not face a late enrollment penalty during this period that he is covered by his employer. However, if he separates from service or retires and is no longer covered by his employer plan, John must enroll in Medicare within the appropriate time frame. John would be eligible for a Special Election Period (SEP): He would have an eight (8) month SEP to sign up for Medicare Part A and/or Part B that begins when either of the following happens first -- (1) The month after employment ends. (2) The month after his group health plan insurance based on current employment ends.

> You must enroll in Medicare Part D immediately when eligible (age 65) or upon retirement to avoid paying late enrollment penalties.

Medicare Part D: How It Works

Whether you have a stand-alone Medicare Prescription Drug Plan or receive Medicare Part D coverage as part of a Medicare Advantage plan, it works in the same way:

- Your plan has a list of covered drugs called a formulary.

- Formulary guidelines are set by CMS (Center for Medicare and Medicaid Services).

- The covered drugs are divided into Tiers (Tiers 1-5).

- Tiers vary based on insurance companies and the drug itself.

- You generally pay the same copay or coinsurance for all the drugs in each specific Tier. However, this can vary. (*Example*: You might pay a $3 copay for a Tier 1 drug, but you might pay a 25% coinsurance for a Tier 4 drug).

- It is imperative to review each individual medication, to determine its Tier and specific costs associated with that Tier.

- Variations amongst companies can be costly.

Medicare Part D: Benefit Stages

Medicare Part D has different stages in benefits, and your coverage may change depending on which stage you're in.

Stage 1: Initial Coverage

- You pay copays or coinsurance for all covered drugs based on which Tier the drug is in.

- You continue to pay these copays until your total drug costs for the year reach the **Initial Coverage Limit (ICL).**

- **Initial Coverage Limit for 2020 is $4,020 compared to 2019 is $3,820 (changes occur annually).**

- Your total drug costs are what is paid by both you and your insurance company.

- Your insurance company will issue monthly statements reflecting what is paid by both parties.

  ❖ **BEWARE:**

  ➢ It is important to review monthly statements to make sure your payments are correct. This also helps with choosing the appropriate plan each year.

Stage 2: Coverage Gap (Donut Hole)

- Many plans **do not** cover prescription drugs in the Coverage Gap.

- However, you pay discounted prices on both brand name and generic drugs.

- During this time, you pay 25% of the plan's cost for brand name drugs and 37% of the plan's cost for generic drugs.

  ❖ **BEWARE:**

  ➢ Some plans do offer drug coverage during the coverage gap.

➢ Make sure that you check your plan's coverage details in order not to be surprised by additional drug costs due to the coverage gap.

Stage 3: Catastrophic Coverage

- **Catastrophic coverage begins once YOUR out of pocket expenses reach $6,350 in 2020 compared to $5,100 in 2019.**

- **Costs paid by your insurance company are not included.**

- Once you have reached the total out of pocket expense of $6,350, you pay either a copayment or coinsurance for your drug costs and your plan pays the rest.

- In 2020, your costs in this stage would be a $3.60 copay for generic drugs and $8.95 copay for brand name drugs **or** 5% coinsurance, **whichever is greater**!

  ❖ **BEWARE:**

  ➢ Costs can vary and can be significant. When you need prescription drug coverage, you want a plan that will cover unforeseen expenses for your medications. Be sure to review your complete list of medications and compare the various Tiers of these drugs on each insurance company's formularies.

Late Enrollment Penalties for Medicare Part D

- The late enrollment penalty is an amount added to your Medicare Part D monthly premium.

- You may owe a late enrollment penalty if, for any continuous 63 days or more after your Initial Enrollment Period is over, you go without one of these:

> A Medicare Prescription Drug Plan (such as Medicare Part D).

> A Medicare Advantage Plan (Medicare Part C, HMO or PPO).

> Another Medicare health plan that offers Medicare prescription drug coverage.

> Creditable prescription drug coverage.

❖ **BEWARE:**

> Extra Help with Medicare Prescription Drug Plan Costs is available to help those who have limited income and resources to pay for the costs - monthly premiums, annual deductibles, and prescription copayments - related to a Medicare prescription drug plan. Those who receive Extra Help do not pay the late enrollment penalty.

- The cost of the late enrollment penalty depends on how long you've been without Medicare Part D or creditable prescription drug coverage.

- Medicare calculates the penalty by multiplying 1% of the "national base beneficiary premium" ($32.74 in 2020) by the number of full, uncovered months you didn't have Medicare Part D or creditable coverage.

❖ **BEWARE:**

> **The Medicare Part D late enrollment penalty is added to your monthly Part D premium.**

> The national base beneficiary premium may increase each year, which means your penalty may also increase.

Part VII

How Healthcare Costs Impact Your Retirement Cash Flow

I t is critical in managing retirement cash flow to summarize and recognize the true cost of Medicare. You must keep in mind two very important factors about healthcare costs in general when determining your retirement planning and cash flow needs.

1. Healthcare costs are continuing to rise significantly.

2. A variety of possible Medicare cost changes may occur each year according to Centers for Medicare & Medicaid Services (CMS).

Your retirement income (Cash Flow) can be significantly affected by these changes both positively or negatively. The average healthcare costs are now approximately 33% (⅓) of your total retirement expenditures.

You must be fully aware of your Medicare costs including Part A, B, C and D as summarized below:

71

1. Medicare Part A – Hospital and Hospice Services

This is what you paid for in payroll taxes throughout your working lifetime. There will be additional costs.

- You may have to pay a monthly premium: $458 if you paid Medicare taxes less than 30 quarters; $252 if you worked more than 30 to 39 quarters.

- You pay a deductible of $1,408 each time you are admitted to a hospital.

- You also pay coinsurance as a hospital patient. There is $0 coinsurance for days 1-60. After 60 days, the cost is $352 a day until day 90. Beginning day 91, the hospital cost increases to $704 for each day. There are "Lifetime Reserve Days" that Original Medicare will pay for when you're in a hospital for more than 90 days. You have a total of 60 Reserve Days that can be used during your lifetime. For each Lifetime Reserve Day, Medicare pays all covered costs except for a daily coinsurance. **Beyond your Lifetime Reserve Days, you are responsible for all costs.**

❖ **BEWARE:**

➢ Medicare Part A only covers you for inpatient benefits if you are admitted to the hospital. You are not eligible just by being seen in an Emergency Room. **ER visits are not covered as an inpatient hospital benefit.** ER visits fall under Medicare Part B and include their own copays and coinsurance.

❖ **BEWARE:**

➢ Your premium can increase 10% if you do not enroll in Medicare when you are first eligible at 65 unless you are still working and have creditable coverage.

2. Medicare Part B – Medical Provider Services

- You pay a monthly premium: $144.60 (or higher depending on income).

- You pay an annual deductible: $198.

- You pay coinsurance: 20% (typically) of Medicare-approved charges.

3. Medicare Part C – Medicare Supplemental and Medicare Advantage Plans

- You pay an additional premium for Supplemental Plans that can be purchased from insurance companies to cover many of the costs of Original Medicare. The amount of the premium depends on the plan purchased. These plans do not include Part D coverage.

- Medicare Advantage Plans provided by private insurance companies under contract to the Federal Government include all parts in one plan (One card can include your combined coverage of Medicare Parts A, B, C and Part D); coverage of Original Medicare coinsurance, and the option to obtain additional coverage benefits. You still pay your costs for Medicare Parts A and B premiums and you pay another premium to the insurance company depending on which Advantage Plan you choose for the additional benefits provided for Medicare Part C and Part D.

4. Medicare Part D – Prescription Drugs

- You pay a monthly premium: $30 average (increases depending on income and plan choices).

- You pay deductibles for higher Tier drugs.

- You pay copays depending on the Tier level of the drugs prescribed.

❖ **BEWARE:**

➢ There are significant price penalties if you do not enroll in Part D for any continuous 63-day period after your Medicare Initial Enrollment Period (a seven-month period that begins three months before you turn 65).

If you are lucky enough not to require any healthcare services in 2020 and you have paid Medicare payroll taxes for at least 10 years, your Original Medicare insurance plan (Medicare Parts A, B and D) for a single person will cost you annually approximately $2,095.20.*

* (Part A = $0, Part B = $144.60/month, Part D = $30/month)

Part A: $0 x 12 months = $0

Part B: $ 144.60 x 12 months = $1,735.20

Part D: $30 x 12 months = $360

Approximate Total Cost = $2,095.20*

Add approximately $5,496 if you paid Medicare taxes for less than 30 quarters (The standard Part A premium is $458 per month x 12 months = $5,496).

OR

Add approximately $3,024 if you paid Medicare taxes for 30-39 quarters (The standard Part A premium is $252 per month x 12 months = $3,024).

You must then **add** your premiums for your Medicare Supplemental Plan and your Prescription Drug Plan (PDP), or your Medicare Advantage Plan.**

** *Reminder: You generally cannot enroll in both a Medicare Advantage plan and a Medicare Supplemental plan simultaneously.*

74

Part VIII

A Real Life Scenario

As mentioned throughout this book, healthcare costs can significantly affect your retirement Cash Flow. Wise retirement planning should include the rising costs of Healthcare, Social Security, and Medicare.

And you just may live longer than you think.

Today, many people base their planning on what their parents and grandparents experienced. However, individual life expectancies have improved dramatically over the past century. The current trend suggests that one out of three (⅓) males and one out of two (½) females who are in their mid-50s today will live to be 90.

The real question is:

Will your retirement income plan (Cash Flow) be enough?

Your Cash Flow is crucial to ensure you do not outlive your money.

Financial Longevity is a must.

Here's Joe's story to provide you with an actual real-life scenario:

When Joe retired, he promptly signed up for Medicare (Parts A, B and D) to avoid penalties. Having paid Medicare payroll taxes for more than 40 years, he paid no premium for Part A; only for Part B at the time. Since he was in reasonably good health, Joe enrolled in a Medicare Advantage Plan (Part C) which included Prescription Drug Coverage (Part D). He paid only a few copays for routine doctor visits and low Tier pharmaceuticals.

Two years later, Joe developed a back problem. He repeatedly saw his primary care doctor and an orthopedic specialist, had numerous x-rays, an MRI and countless physical therapy visits. Joe was responsible for many copays at the rate of $20 - $50 per visit. The most expensive charge was for the MRI, and Joe was surprised by its cost: an additional $200.

Throughout the first six months of the year Joe's total out-of-pocket medical expenses (deductibles, coinsurance and copays) were $2,000. That total was less than half of his so-called annual in-network, maximum out-of-pocket cost of $5,000. His insurance company and providers reported the expenses to him, but like many, Joe unfortunately ignored the report or was not sure what it meant for him.

A Costly Surprise

Joe had a costly surprise after he learned that he needed extensive back surgery. Based on the calculations in Original Medicare Part A and B, Joe may have been responsible for 20% of the bill, which in this case had a total overall cost of $50,000. 20% of the bill would have been $10,000 in coinsurance.

However, the good news was that Joe had a current Medicare Advantage Plan. Based on Joe's estimates for surgery in his home state, these costs were capped at the in-network, maximum out-of-pocket costs of $5,000.

As stated previously, Joe had only spent $2,000 on his medical throughout the year. Joe was responsible for the difference between his in-network, maximum out of pocket costs ($5,000) less the amount spent throughout the year ($2,000). His total cost, if the surgery was completed in his home state, was going to be approximately $3,000.

Panic set in as Joe realized that he would be personally responsible for paying the remaining $3,000 if the surgery was completed in his home state. This discovery prompted Joe to ask questions since he was interested in possibly having the surgery in another state.

Joe soon learned that if he chose to have surgery in a different state, he would be responsible for the unpaid balance of the out-of-network maximum of $10,000, which was separate from his in-network maximum out-of-pocket costs currently of $5,000.

This was a significant difference for Joe, who was unaware that the out-of-network maximum out-of-pocket limit ($10,000) for another state was separate from his in-network maximum out-of-pocket limit ($5,000). All services he had done in Rhode Island would not count toward the out-of-network maximum limit. These were two separate areas and responsibilities.

Furthermore, because of his back surgery and related problems, Joe was prescribed several high Tier pharmaceuticals. These prescriptions triggered a one-time deductible under Medicare Part D, along with many high copays for his prescriptions monthly. Joe's total Medicare costs for that year more than tripled. He was forced to take additional money from his retirement plans to pay for these expenses, which in turn caused a snowball effect.

He was surprised to learn that he would owe significant taxes to the IRS when his income tax return was filed due to his retirement distributions. Joe was also shocked to learn that due to his Modified Adjusted Gross Income (MAGI) he now had to pay additional Part B and Part D Income Related Monthly Adjustment Amounts (IRMAA) due to these retirement plan withdrawals.

Not only would these tax implications impact Joe in the current tax year but future years as well. The IRMAA would continue to affect his cash flow monthly for the next two years.

Rising Healthcare Costs

From this point on, Joe's healthcare costs continued to rise and be higher than when he initially had turned 65 and was in reasonably good health. So, too, did his tax consequences for the next two years and the overall costs of his Medicare premium costs.

It is imperative to determine the best healthcare plan for your current and future healthcare needs. You must be cognizant that unexpected health issues may arise. Each individual is different, and you must evaluate your specific health concerns to determine the best plan for you. Annually, Medicare plans and costs vary and continue to be on the rise. These rising healthcare costs, over many years, have and will continue to affect your cash flow needs throughout your retirement.

In addition, it is crucial to review your tax, financial and retirement planning to ensure that income levels are controlled and do not cause you to rise above set Modified Adjusted Gross Income (MAGI) limits which will in turn be costly.

Keep in mind, you must remember that the look-back period for MAGI - your total Modified Adjusted Gross Income and tax-exempt interest income - is two years. Be conscious of the trend that IRMAA represents today on Part B and Part D of Medicare. Costs continue to rise, and eligibility income levels (income tax brackets for what you are responsible to pay) can be expected to drop in the future years.

Proper planning and Cash Flow are imperative to your retirement planning to ensure Financial Longevity.

By understanding the various Medicare plans, you can plan better than Joe did and not have additional surprises.

Part IX

Epilogue

s you now have learned, Social Security and Medicare have numerous moving parts, complex rules and continuous changes.

Understanding it all is not easy.

We hope that after reading *Medicare Untangled*, the Medicare process has been simplified and that you have a better understanding of its complexities.

As you continue to sort through Medicare's vast number of moving parts, please utilize *Medicare Untangled* as a reference and a guide for your Medicare needs.

Should you have any questions or would like additional information visit us at **www.Universalwm.com** or contact the experts at **UWM: 401-331-7600**.

Part X

Glossary of Commonly Used Healthcare Acronyms

ACA	**Affordable Care Act**
AEP	**Annual Election Period**
CCP	**Coordinated Care Plans**
CHIP	**Children's Health Insurance Program**
CMS	**Centers for Medicare and Medicaid Services**
COB	**Coordination of Benefits**

COBRA	**Consolidated Omnibus Budget Reconciliation Act**
COLA	**Cost of Living Adjustment**
DME	**Durable Medical Equipment**
EHR	**Electronic Health Records**
EOB	**Explanation of Benefits**
EPO	**Exclusive Provider Organization**
ESRD	**End-Stage Renal Disease**
FFS	**Fee-For-Service**
FEHBP	**Federal Employee Health Benefits Program**
FPL	**Federal Poverty Level**
FSA	**Flexible Spending Account**
HCR	**Health Care Reform**

HCBS	**Home and Community-Based Services**
HHS	**U.S. Department of Health and Human Services**
HIPAA	**Health Insurance Portability and Accountability Act**
HIM/HIX	**Health Insurance Marketplace / Health Insurance Exchange**
HMO	**Health Maintenance Organization**
HSA	**Health Savings Account**
HDHP	**High Deductible Health Plan**
ICEP	**Initial Coverage Election Period**
ICL	**Initial Coverage Limit**
IEP	**Initial Enrollment Period**
IRMAA	**Income Related Monthly Adjustment Amount**
LEP	**Late Enrollment Penalty**

LIS	Low Income Subsidy
LTC	Long-Term Care
LTD	Long-Term Disability
MAGI	Modified Adjusted Gross Income
MA	Medicare Advantage
MA-PD	Medicare Advantage – Prescription Drug
MOOP	Maximum Out of Pocket
MSA	Medical Savings Account
NDC	National Drug Code
OASDI	Old-Age, Survivors and Disability Insurance
OEP	Open Enrollment Period
OEPI	Open Enrollment Period for Institutionalized Individuals

OON	Out-of-Network
OOP	Out-of-Pocket
OTC	Over the Counter
PBM	Pharmacy Benefit Management
PEC	Pre-existing Condition
PCIP	Pre-existing Condition Insurance Plan
PCMH	Patient-Centered Medical Home
PCP	Primary Care Provider
PFFS	Private Fee-For-Service
PDP	Prescription Drug Plan under Medicare Part D
POS	Point-of-Service Plan
PPO	Preferred Provider Organization

QHP	**Qualified Health Plan**
SBC	**Summary of Benefits and Coverage**
SEP	**Special Election Period** **Special Enrollment Period**
SHIP	**State Health Insurance** **Assistance Program**
SMI	**Supplemental Medical Insurance**
SNF	**Skilled Nursing Facility**
SNP	**Special Needs Plan**
SPP	**Specialty Pharmacy Provider**
STD	**Short-Term Disability**
SSDI	**Social Security Disability Income**
SSP	**State Supplementary Payment**
SSI	**Supplemental Security Income**

Karen Emma
Universal Wealth Management | President | Founding Partner
Registered Financial Advisor | Independent Insurance Agent

For 20 years, Karen has been a successful wealth management leader, providing clients with personalized investment advice and pioneering retirement planning inclusive of Social Security, Healthcare and Medicare to help secure Financial Longevity©.

After graduating from Brown University with degrees in Business, Entrepreneurship and Psychology, Karen began her finance career providing tailored investment advice at Smith Barney in Providence, RI. After nearly a decade with the company, Karen went off on her own and launched Universal Wealth Management, LLC, dedicated to providing a broad approach to Financial Longevity©.

Karen has a proven track record for providing sound financial guidance to her clients through many major life transitions in areas including Social Security and understanding the complexities of all aspects of Medicare (Individuals and Businesses), Prescription Drug Coverage and Individual and Group Health Care Plans.

UWM today successfully provides personal, family, business, estate, healthcare and career financial advice and management to more than 500 households and manages in excess of $250 million in assets. Additionally, Karen is a registered representative with Royal Alliance Associates, Inc., a prominent independent, full service broker-dealer.

Karen's drive as a businesswoman stems from her competitive nature as a former standout athlete: A rare two-sport student-athlete at Boston College and Brown University where she excelled in both women's hockey and softball. As a senior at Brown, Karen achieved the unique distinction of winning both ECAC and Ivy League titles in hockey (22-0-0 ECAC and 10-0-0 in Ivy) and capturing the Ivy League Softball Championship. She also was a member of the United States Olympic Hockey Development Program.

She has continued her participation in sports today. She coaches both youth hockey and baseball and formerly served as the head hockey coach of her alma mater, St. Mary Academy Bay View. Under Karen's direction, BV won three state championships and was the state runner-ups four times. Karen had been honored as the RI Schoolgirl Coach of the Year and has been inducted in Bay View's Athletic Hall of Fame. The RI Interscholastic League celebrated Karen's accomplishments by naming its top hockey division The Emma Division.

Karen was honored as one of the top businesswomen in Rhode Island by *Providence Business News* in 2017.

A Rhode Island native, Karen resides in Cranston, RI, with her son Edward L. Walsh III.

Attributions:

1. "Home." *CMS.gov Centers for Medicare & Medicaid Services*, 23 Feb. 2019, www.cms.gov.
2. eHealth Insurance. "EHealth Is America's #1 Private Health Insurance Site." *EHealth Insurance Resource Center*, EHealth Insurance, 15 Nov. 2018, www.ehealthinsurance.com.
3. "Get 2019 Health Coverage. Health Insurance Marketplace." *HealthCare.gov*, www.healthcare.gov.
4. U.S. Department of Health and Human Services. (n.d.). HHS.gov. Retrieved from www.hhs.gov.
5. "Immune Deficiency Foundation." *Other Primary Cellular Immunodeficiencies | Immune Deficiency Foundation*, www.primaryimmune.org.
6. "The Official U.S. Government Site for Medicare." *Medicare.gov - the Official U.S. Government Site for Medicare*, www.medicare.gov.
7. Dictionary by Merriam-Webster: America's most-trusted online dictionary. (n.d.). Retrieved from www.merriam-webster.com.
8. "Social Security." *Reports, Facts and Figures | Press Office| Social Security Administration*, Social Security Administration, www.ssa.gov.
9. The Balance. (2018, January 08). Retrieved from www.thebalance.com.
10. Social Security Disability. Secrets & Advice to Win Benefits. Apply & Appeal SSDI & SSI. (n.d.). Retrieved from www.disabilitysecrets.com.

These materials are provided for general information and educational purposes based upon publicly available information from sources believed to be reliable - we cannot assure the accuracy or completeness of these materials. The information in these materials may change at any time and without notice.